# The *Skin* You're In

To order additional copies of this book, contact:
Xlibris
844-714-8691
www.Xlibris.com
Orders@Xlibris.com

ISBN:   Softcover           978-1-6698-0805-3
        EBook               978-1-6698-0804-6

Print information available on the last page

Rev. date: 02/23/2022

# The Skin You're In

# Dedication

I dedicate this book to my family for being a great influence in my life. For sharing the personal experiences with me regarding to colorism that exists in our communities, that needs to stop. So that there can be more harmony and peace in the world. Love yall.

Your skin is beautiful.
Light skin, brown skin, dark skin.
Were are all the same.

The Skin You're In.

Brothers and sisters your ancestors was kings and queens.
Don't lower your standards acting as a peasant hurting one another.
But instead give a lending hand to help your brother.
Dont be a puppet on a string.

The Skin You're In

You possess the qualities of our past higher beings.
My sister, my brother let's unite with each other.
And love one another.
There is none like us and will be no other.

The Skin You're In.

Baby hold your head high
stick out your chest.
No matter what shade you are
you're just as good as the rest.

The Skin You're In

Just as our ancestors walk in pride and dignity
For this is the success remedy.
There is room for everyone
For everyone to succeed
Look at your skin
And mine Im not your enemy.

The Skin You're In.

Even though life can be hard
Hard like a test
Fix your crown
And always remember
The melanin that you have
Many wish they possessed

The Skin You're In

The End